P9-CAN-185

Bluetooth

Cristie Reed

Educational Media

rourkeeducationalmedia.com

*Scan for Related Titles
and Teacher Resources*

Teaching Focus:
Text feature: Diagrams- How do the diagrams help you understand the information in the text?

Before Reading:

Building Academic Vocabulary and Background Knowledge
Before reading a book, it is important to set the stage for your child or student by using pre-reading strategies. This will help them develop their vocabulary, increase their reading comprehension, and make connections across the curriculum.
1. *Read the title and look at the cover. Let's make predictions about what this book will be about.*
2. *Take a picture walk by talking about the pictures/photographs in the book. Implant the vocabulary as you take the picture walk. Be sure to talk about the text features such as headings, Table of Contents, glossary, bolded words, captions, charts/ diagrams, or Index.*
3. Have students read the first page of text with you then have students read the remaining text.
4. *Strategy Talk – use to assist students while reading.*
   - *Get your mouth ready*
   - *Look at the picture*
   - *Think…does it make sense*
   - *Think…does it look right*
   - *Think…does it sound right*
   - *Chunk it – by looking for a part you know*
5. *Read it again.*
6. *After reading the book complete the activities below.*

Content Area Vocabulary
Use glossary words in a sentence.

convenience
device
mobile
network
radio waves
synchronize

After Reading:

Comprehension and Extension Activity
After reading the book, work on the following questions with your child or students in order to check their level of reading comprehension and content mastery.
1. *How have Bluetooth devices changed the way we stay healthy, use our cell phones, or get information? (Asking questions)*
2. *Explain what synchronize means. (Summarize)*
3. *What are some ways you have used a Bluetooth device? (Text to self connection)*
4. *How does a Bluetooth device connect to other devices? (Summarize)*

Extension Activity
Think about all the computers, tablets, printers, smartphones, and gaming systems you have at home. Now cut a 4 foot (1.22 meter) piece of string to represent each device you have. Tape all the strings on your desk so they hang to the floor. What does it look like? How could all the cords become a problem on a desk or in a single area? How does Bluetooth help?

Table of Contents

What Is Bluetooth?

Bluetooth technology allows electronic devices to connect without cables or wires. You can find Bluetooth in **mobile** phones, computers, medical devices, and home entertainment devices.

 Bluetooth™

Bluetooth was named for a tenth century Danish King named Harald Bluetooth.

How Does Bluetooth Help Us?

Bluetooth adds **convenience** to the products we use every day.

Usually, devices are connected with cables or wires. But cords get tangled and take up space on your desk.

Bluetooth replaces the cables, making devices easier to use and more mobile.

Bluetooth In Our Lives

A mobile phone with Bluetooth connects to a car radio or mobile device. The driver can make phone calls without taking his or her eyes off the road.

Hands-free talking with Bluetooth makes driving safer.

Smartphones and tablets **synchronize** with your computer over Bluetooth. A home computer may connect to a wireless mouse.

Without wires, game controls can go anywhere in the room.

Bluetooth radio waves can travel through objects and walls. If they are close enough, they can connect.

Healthcare workers use Bluetooth to keep track of their patients' heart rate and breathing. Patients wear monitors that send information to a computer or smartphone.

Athletes use Bluetooth monitors to improve their performance. They can check their heart rate and keep track of their workouts.

How Does Bluetooth Work?

Bluetooth devices use **radio waves** to connect. The radio waves come from a small computer chip.

When one Bluetooth **device** comes close to another Bluetooth device, they send out radio signals to each other.

One Bluetooth device can communicate with any other Bluetooth device. They just have to be close together.

Most Bluetooth devices have a range of about 30 feet (10 meters).

The devices connect and create a personal area **network** (PAN). The devices share information. Voices, music, photos, videos, and data can travel through the network.

Computer

Wireless
sound

Bluetooth
devices

Other

Health
monitors

19

Bluetooth is making the devices we use every day work smarter.

Photo Glossary

convenience (kuhn-VEEN-yuhns): Something that makes life easier.

device (duh-VIS): A tool or machine that performs a task.

mobile (MO-buhl): Easy to move from place to place.

 **network** (net-WURK): A group of things that communicate with each other and work together.

 **radio waves** (ray-DEE-o wavs): Invisible waves for sending sound and images.

 **synchronize** (sing-KROH-niz): To match information and files.

Index

Websites to Visit

www.sciencekids.co.nz

www.inventionatplay.org

www.engineergirl.org

Meet The Author!
www.meetREMauthors.com

About the Author

Cristie Reed has been a teacher for many years. She lives in Florida with her husband and pet dog, Rocky. She hopes technology can help kids learn to read and can help them enjoy reading more.

© 2015 Rourke Educational Media

www.rourkeeducationalmedia.com

PHOTO CREDITS: Cover © MikeA, chictype; title page © skynesher; page 5 © BirgerNiss; page 7, 22 © Derek Latta; page 9, 22 © Darrenbaker; page 10 © George Doyle; page 11 © SerrNovik; page 12, 23 © Andriy Popov; page 13 © nattrass; page 15, 23 © Angel Simon; page 17 © gchutkapage 19 © petekarici, Amorphis, monticello, You Can More; peresanz, arsenik, duckycards, chiryacat, angeloNZ; page 21, 22 © Tom Wang;

Edited by: Jill Sherman

Cover and Interior design by: Jen Thomas

Library of Congress PCN Data

Bluetooth/ Cristie Reed
(How It Works)
ISBN (hard cover)(alk. paper) 978-1-62717-645-3
ISBN (soft cover) 978-1-62717-767-2
ISBN (e-Book) 978-1-62717-887-7
Library of Congress Control Number: 2014934237
Printed in the United States of America, North Mankato, Minnesota

Also Available as: